YOUTH SERVICES

YOUTH SERVICES

Creepy Creatures

Pill Bugs

Monica Hughes

Raintree

Chicago, Illinois

© 2004 Raintree
Published by Raintree, a division of Reed Elsevier, Inc.
Chicago, Illinois
Customer Service 888-363-4266
Visit our website at www.raintreelibrary.com

For information, address the publisher:
Raintree, 100 N. LaSalle, Suite 1200, Chicago, IL 60602

Printed and bound in the United States at Lake Book Manufacturing, Inc.
07 06 05 04 03
10 9 8 7 6 5 4 3 2 1

Library of Congress Cataloging-in-Publication Data:
Hughes, Monica.
  Pill bugs / Monica Hughes.
     p. cm. -- (Creepy creatures)
Includes bibliographical references and index.
Contents: Pill bugs -- Looking for pill bugs -- A pill bug's body --
Body parts -- Young pill bugs -- Growing up -- Food for pill bugs --
Pill bugs in danger -- Pill bugs in winter.
  ISBN 1-4109-0624-8 (lib. bdg.); 1-4109-0650-7 (pbk.)
  1. Isopoda--Juvenile literature. [1. Wood lice (Crustaceans)] I.
Title. II. Series: Hughes, Monica. Creepy creatures.
  QL444.M34H84 2003
  595.3'72--dc21
                          2003008570

Acknowledgments
The Publishers would like to thank the following for permission to reproduce photographs: pp. 16, 20
Heather Angel; p. 23 Ardea: Jean-Paul Ferrero, pp. 4/5, 10, 17, 19, 22a, 22b Steve Hopkin; p. 21 BBC
NHU: Dan Burton; p. 15 Duncan McEwan; p. 6 BBC NHU/Premaphotos; pp. 12, 13 Bruce Coleman:
Dwight Kuhn; pp. 11, 14 NHPA: NA Callon; p. 18 Stephen Dalton; p. 7 Oxford Scientific Films; pp. 8/9
Scott Camazine, John Cooke

Cover photograph reproduced with permission of Ardea/Steve Hopkin

Some words are shown in bold, **like this.** You can find out
what they mean by looking in the glossary on page 24.

Contents

Pill Bugs

Pill bugs are small animals.

They are **invertebrates**.

Kinds of Pill Bugs

There are about 40 kinds of pill bugs.
All pill bugs look a lot alike.

Crabs and shrimp
are pill bug cousins.

crab

shrimp

Looking at Pill Bugs

segment

Pill bugs have hard bodies.
Their bodies have **segments.**

Pill Bug Parts

Grown-up pill bugs have seven **pairs** of legs.

Pill bugs have **antennae,** too.

Looking for Pill Bugs

Pill bugs live in dark, damp places.

You might see them at night under logs or in dead leaves.

Hatching

A **female** pill bug lays eggs.

The eggs **hatch**.

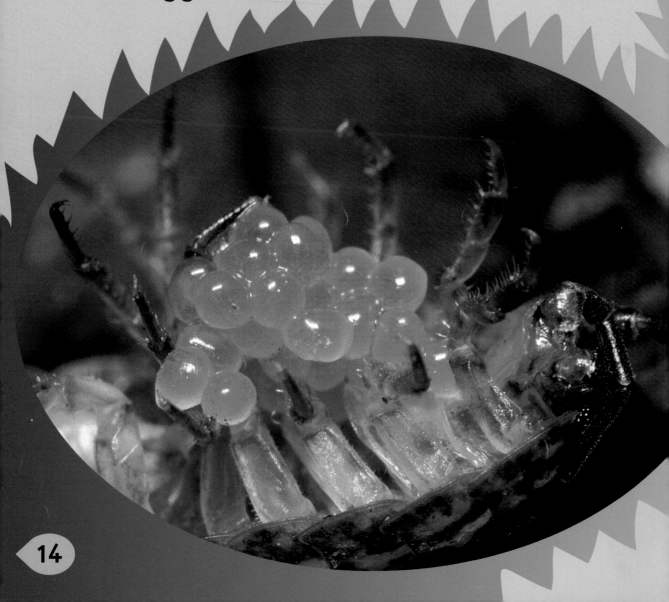

Baby pill bugs have soft,
white bodies.

They have six **pairs** of legs.

Growing

A young pill bug grows.
It **sheds** the back part of its shell.

After a few days, it sheds the front part of its shell.

A new shell is underneath.

Food for Pill Bugs

tree bark

mushrooms

Pill bugs eat dead plants.
They eat mushrooms
and tree bark, too.

Sometimes they eat shells other pill bugs **shed**.

Pill Bugs in Danger!

Frogs and lizards look for pill bugs to eat.

A pill bug can roll into a hard ball to hide from danger.

Pill Bugs in Winter

Pill bugs do not move around in winter.

They hide under stones or logs.
They wake up when the weather
gets warm.

23

Glossary

antenna (You say an-TEN-uh. More than one are antennae.) feelers on an insect's head that help it smell, see, or hear

female girl pill bug

hatch to come out of an egg

invertebrate animal without bones

pair two things that are alike and that go together

segment part or section

shed to drop off

Index